Francis Frith's

Dorset
Living Memories

PHOTOGRAPHIC MEMORIES

Francis Frith's
Dorset
Living Memories

John Bainbridge

First published in the United Kingdom in 2000 by
Frith Book Company Ltd

Paperback edition 2002
Reprinted in Paperback 2004

British Library Cataloguing in Publication Data

Dorset Living Memories
John Bainbridge
ISBN 1-85937-584-7

Frith Book Company Ltd
Frith's Barn, Teffont,
Salisbury, Wiltshire SP3 5QP
Tel: +44 (0) 1722 716 376
Fax: +44 (0) 1722 716 881
Email: info@francisfrith.co.uk
Web Site: www.francisfrith.co.uk

Printed and bound in Great Britain

Front Cover: WEYMOUTH, The Beach c1955 W76098

The colour-tinting is for illustrative purposes only, and is not intended to be historically accurate

AS WITH ANY HISTORICAL DATABASE THE FRITH ARCHIVE IS CONSTANTLY BEING CORRECTED AND IMPROVED
AND THE PUBLISHERS WOULD WELCOME INFORMATION ON OMISSIONS OR INACCURACIES

Contents

Francis Frith: *Victorian Pioneer*

FRANCIS FRITH, Victorian founder of the world-famous photographic archive, was a complex and multitudinous man. A devout Quaker and a highly successful Victorian businessman, he was both philosophical by nature and pioneering in outlook.

By 1855 Francis Frith had already established a wholesale grocery business in Liverpool, and sold it for the astonishing sum of £200,000, which is the equivalent today of over £15,000,000. Now a multi-millionaire, he was able to indulge his passion for travel. As a child he had pored over travel books written by early explorers, and his fancy and imagination had been stirred by family holidays to the sublime mountain regions of Wales and Scotland. 'What a land of spirit-stirring and enriching scenes and places!' he had written. He was to return to these scenes of grandeur in later years to 'recapture the thousands of vivid and tender memories', but with a different purpose. Now in his thirties, and captivated by the new science of photography, Frith set out on a series of pioneering journeys to the Nile regions that occupied him from 1856 until 1860.

Intrigue and Adventure

He took with him on his travels a specially-designed wicker carriage that acted as both dark-room and sleeping chamber. These far-flung journeys were packed with intrigue and adventure. In his life story, written when he was sixty-three, Frith tells of being held captive by bandits, and of fighting 'an awful midnight battle to the very point of surrender with a deadly pack of hungry, wild dogs'. Sporting flowing Arab costume, Frith arrived at Akaba by camel sixty years before Lawrence, where he encountered 'desert princes and rival sheikhs, blazing with jewel-hilted swords'.

During these extraordinary adventures he was assiduously exploring the desert regions bordering the Nile and patiently recording the antiquities and peoples with his camera. He was the first photographer to venture beyond the sixth cataract. Africa was still the mysterious 'Dark Continent', and Stanley and Livingstone's historic meeting was a decade into the future. The conditions for picture taking confound belief. He laboured for hours in his wicker dark-room in the sweltering heat of the desert, while the volatile chemicals fizzed dangerously in their trays. Often he was forced to work in remote tombs and caves where conditions were cooler. Back in London he exhibited his photographs and was 'rapturously cheered' by members of the Royal Society. His reputation as a photographer was made overnight. An eminent modern historian has likened their impact on the population of the time to that on our own generation of the first photographs taken on the surface of the moon.

Venture of a Life-Time

Characteristically, Frith quickly spotted the opportunity to create a new business as a specialist publisher of photographs. He lived in an era of immense and sometimes violent change. For the poor in the early part of Victoria's reign work was a drudge and the hours long, and people had precious little free time to enjoy themselves. Most had no transport other than a cart or gig at their disposal, and had not travelled far beyond the boundaries of their own town or village.

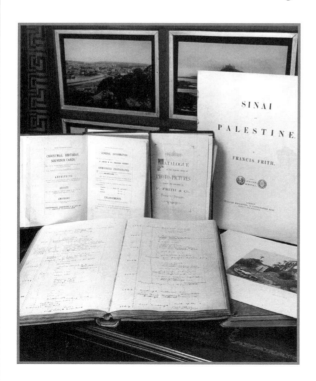

However, by the 1870s, the railways had threaded their way across the country, and Bank Holidays and half-day Saturdays had been made obligatory by Act of Parliament. All of a sudden the ordinary working man and his family were able to enjoy days out and see a little more of the world.

With characteristic business acumen, Francis Frith foresaw that these new tourists would enjoy having souvenirs to commemorate their days out. In 1860 he married Mary Ann Rosling and set out with the intention of photographing every city, town and village in Britain. For the next thirty years he travelled the country by train and by pony and trap, producing fine photographs of seaside resorts and beauty spots that were keenly bought by millions of Victorians. These prints were painstakingly pasted into family albums and pored over during the dark nights of winter, rekindling precious memories of summer excursions.

The Rise of Frith & Co

Frith's studio was soon supplying retail shops all over the country. To meet the demand he gathered about him a small team of photographers, and published the work of independent artist-photographers of the calibre of Roger Fenton and Francis Bedford. In order to gain some understanding of the scale of Frith's business one only has to look at the catalogue issued by Frith & Co in 1886: it runs to some 670 pages, listing not only many thousands of views of the British Isles but also many photographs of most European countries, and China, Japan, the USA and Canada – note the sample page shown on page 9

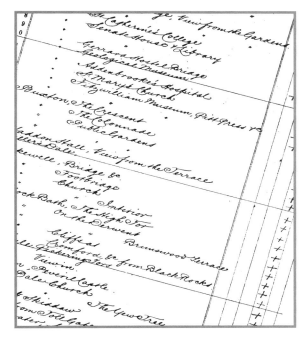

from the hand-written *Frith & Co* ledgers detailing pictures taken. By 1890 Frith had created the greatest specialist photographic publishing company in the world, with over 2,000 outlets – more than the combined number that Boots and WH Smith have today! The picture on the right shows the *Frith & Co* display board at Ingleton in the Yorkshire Dales (left of window). Beautifully constructed with a mahogany frame and gilt inserts, it could display up to a dozen local scenes.

Postcard Bonanza

The ever-popular holiday postcard we know today took many years to develop. In 1870 the Post Office issued the first plain cards, with a pre-printed stamp on one face. In 1894 they allowed other publishers' cards to be sent through the mail with an attached adhesive halfpenny stamp. Demand grew rapidly, and in 1895 a new size of postcard was permitted

called the court card, but there was little room for illustration. In 1899, a year after Frith's death, a new card measuring 5.5 x 3.5 inches became the standard format, but it was not until 1902 that the divided back came into being, with address and message on one face and a full-size illustration on the other. *Frith & Co* were in the vanguard of postcard development, and Frith's sons Eustace and Cyril continued their father's monumental task, expanding the number of views offered to the public and recording more and more places in Britain, as the coasts and countryside were opened up to mass travel.

Francis Frith died in 1898 at his villa in Cannes, his great project still growing. The archive he created continued in business for another seventy years. By 1970 it contained over a third of a million pictures of 7,000 cities, towns and villages. The massive photographic record Frith has left to us stands as a living monument to a special and very remarkable man.

Frith's Archive: *A Unique Legacy*

FRANCIS FRITH'S legacy to us today is of immense significance and value, for the magnificent archive of evocative photographs he created provides a unique record of change in 7,000 cities, towns and villages throughout Britain over a century and more. Frith and his fellow studio photographers revisited locations many times down the years to update their views, compiling for us an enthralling and colourful pageant of British life and character.

We tend to think of Frith's sepia views of Britain as nostalgic, for most of us use them to conjure up memories of places in our own lives with which we have family associations. It often makes us forget that to Francis Frith they were records of daily life as it was actually being lived in the cities, towns and villages of his day. The Victorian age was one of great and often bewildering change for ordinary people, and though the pictures evoke an impression of slower times, life was as busy and hectic as it is today.

We are fortunate that Frith was a photographer of the people, dedicated to recording the minutiae of everyday life. For it is this sheer wealth of visual data, the painstaking chronicle of changes in dress, transport, street layouts, buildings, housing, engineering and landscape that captivates us so much today. His remarkable images offer us a powerful link with the past and with the lives of our ancestors.

Today's Technology

Computers have now made it possible for Frith's many thousands of images to be accessed almost instantly. In the Frith archive today, each photograph is carefully 'digitised' then stored on a CD Rom. Frith archivists can locate a single photograph amongst thousands within seconds. Views can be catalogued and sorted under a variety of categories of place and content to the immediate benefit of researchers.

Inexpensive reference prints can be created for them at the touch of a mouse button, and a wide range of books and other printed materials assembled and published for a wider, more general readership - in the next twelve months over a hundred Frith local history titles will be published! The day-to-day workings of the archive are very different from how they were in Francis Frith's time: imagine the herculean task of sorting through eleven tons of glass negatives as Frith had to do to locate a particular sequence

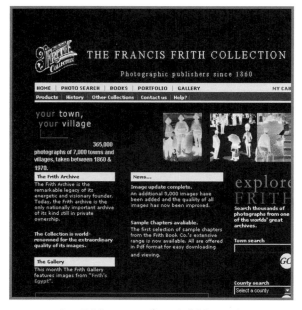

See Frith at www.francisfrith.co.uk

of pictures! Yet the archive still prides itself on maintaining the same high standards of excellence laid down by Francis Frith, including the painstaking cataloguing and indexing of every view.

It is curious to reflect on how the internet now allows researchers in America and elsewhere greater instant access to the archive than Frith himself ever enjoyed. Many thousands of individual views can be called up on screen within seconds on one of the Frith internet sites, enabling people living continents away to revisit the streets of their ancestral home town, or view places in Britain where they have enjoyed holidays. Many overseas researchers welcome the chance to view special theme selections, such as transport, sports, costume and ancient monuments.

We are certain that Francis Frith would have heartily approved of these modern developments in imaging techniques, for he himself was always working at the very limits of Victorian photographic technology.

The Value of the Archive Today

Because of the benefits brought by the computer, Frith's images are increasingly studied by social historians, by researchers into genealogy and ancestory, by architects, town planners, and by teachers and schoolchildren involved in local history projects.

In addition, the archive offers every one of us an opportunity to examine the places where we and our families have lived and worked down the years. Highly successful in Frith's own era, the archive is now, a century and more on, entering a new phase of popularity.

The Past in Tune with the Future

Historians consider the Francis Frith Collection to be of prime national importance. It is the only archive of its kind remaining in private ownership and has been valued at a million pounds. However, this figure is now rapidly increasing as digital technology enables more and more people around the world to enjoy its benefits.

Francis Frith's archive is now housed in an historic timber barn in the beautiful village of Teffont in Wiltshire. Its founder would not recognize the archive office as it is today. In place of the many thousands of dusty boxes containing glass plate negatives and an all-pervading odour of photographic chemicals, there are now ranks of computer screens. He would be amazed to watch his images travelling round the world at unimaginable speeds through network and internet lines.

The archive's future is both bright and exciting. Francis Frith, with his unshakeable belief in making photographs available to the greatest number of people, would undoubtedly approve of what is being done today with his lifetime's work. His photographs, depicting our shared past, are now bringing pleasure and enlightenment to millions around the world a century and more after his death.

Dorset Living Memories
An Introduction

THE 20TH CENTURY has been kinder to Dorset than to many English counties. As we pass along its narrow lanes, explore its enticing villages, or walk across its downlands on ridge paths almost as old as time, we are still seeing a county not so very different to the pastoral Dorset vividly depicted by Thomas Hardy in his immortal series of novels and poems.

Dorset has managed to resist the greater developments that have engulfed so many other counties in southern England. Smaller developments have been absorbed: towns and villages may have increased in size since the majority of these photographs were taken in the 1950s and 1960s, but they have kept their essential character despite an increase in population. Perhaps the greatest intrusion was the moving of Bournemouth and Christchurch into Dorset from neighbouring Hampshire in the

1970s. Bournemouth and Poole now make up one of the largest urban conurbations in the south country, a concept that would have been unimaginable to earlier generations, who would have considered Weymouth and Dorchester to have been large country towns.

Tourism has increased dramatically with the huge growth in car ownership; today the lanes of Dorset are seldom as quiet as shown here, though the pictures are themselves deceptive, for the photographers would probably have waited for the quietest possible moment before closing the shutter. Even in the 1950s, motor cars were getting everywhere. Nevertheless, for those travellers and residents who care to seek out the peaceful places, Dorset retains the atmosphere of a less-hurried age. It is hard to name another English county that has emerged from the 20th century so untainted by what has been called the 'Age of Rush'.

In recent years, Dorset has often been caught pretending that it still is in the past for the benefit of film directors and television companies. The pleasant climate, and the fact that set designers can so easily transform Dorset communities, has demonstrated how little has really changed since earlier centuries. Thus, Lyme Regis has served as the location for a couple of versions of Jane Austen's 'Persuasion', which is set in the town. And who can forget the actress Meryl Streep's brooding presence on Lyme's Cobb, pretending to be 'The French Lieutenant's Woman'? Several classic novels by Thomas Hardy have been made in the county, including a memorable 'Far From the Madding Crowd', with Julie Christie and Peter Finch, filmed at several locations pictured in this book, and 'The Mayor of Casterbridge' with Alan Bates, which was shot in Corfe Castle, as the streets of Dorchester were too busy at the time.

Culture and traditional attractions are everywhere, for Dorset has never been just a place for days on the beach and similar easy attractions. In Dorset it is still possible to spend an amusing afternoon exploring towns laid out in Roman, Saxon or medieval street patterns, or to admire churches built by worshippers a thousand years ago. This is the place to listen to concerts by the world-renowned Bournemouth Symphony Orchestra, or to stroll in the fictional footsteps of Thomas Hardy's characters - who at times seem to have more reality than the residents pictured in these photographs. A 'Hardy Way' long-distance footpath crosses the county, taking the rambler on a long walk from Bockhampton, where the writer was born, to Stinsford where his heart was buried in 1928. This circuitous route through the landscape of the novels passes through many of the places featured in this book.

For the walker interested in the coves and beaches of the dramatic coastline, there is the Dorset Coastal Footpath, which threads above the shoreline linking coastal resorts to old smuggling villages between Lyme Regis and Poole Harbour. A continuation beyond the Studland Ferry takes the coastal walker along the seashores of Bournemouth and historic Christchurch, to the point where Hampshire now begins. This was the land of the fisherman and the quarry worker, and these industries still survive. A stroll around Lyme, or West Bay, when the fishing boats are coming into harbour, is still a spectacle that will never be forgotten, for here is an industry that has survived, with mixed fortunes, for thousands of years. Weymouth is still a substantial port, with boats setting out for the Channel Islands and Continent on most days. Bournemouth is pure holiday resort, and a part of the childhood memories of the millions of Britons who built sandcastles on its lovely beaches. Some experiences are with us forever, and time has mellowed the bitter and unpleasant days.

Within the living memory of the oldest residents are the dangers and disruptions of World War Two, when Dorset represented the British front line for several years - a threat not experienced here since the heyday of Napoleon Bonaparte 140 years earlier. Air raids were common during those dark hours, but it was from such ports as Weymouth that armies of liberation set out to invade Normandy on D-Day. Perhaps the saddest monument in Dorset to 20th-century warfare is the ruined village of Tyneham, taken from its villagers for military training and never returned to them. Thousands more acres are still used for battle-training, and the guns still roar over coast and downland on firing days, though public access has improved in recent years, when the army is not there. Perhaps one day these lands will be freed from duty and dedicated to nature conservation, so that the walker and rider may enjoy them at all times.

A dramatic change between the Dorset of yesteryear and the Dorset of today is the considerable increase in motor traffic. Dorset suffered a great deal from the railway cuts of the past half-century, leaving little alternative but to use car or coach. A glance at these photographs shows how relatively car-free some streets were; though motorists did discover some beauty spots very early on, as we can see from the picture of Lulworth Cove. However, in recent years the major towns, and the villages near to main roads, have found cars to be a considerable burden, though the passengers are welcomed as warmly as ever. Valiant efforts are being made by town and county planners to ensure that visitors to Dorset do not inadvertently destroy the very beauty and tranquillity that they came to enjoy in the first place, but there are no easy answers.

The photographs in this collection show changes within the holiday tradition itself. Bucket and spade seaside holidays remained popular throughout the last century, and still are today, as a glance along Weymouth Sands or Bournemouth's several miles of beaches will show. However, the way they are enjoyed has changed. A number of the old seaside hotels, seen in all their splendour in photographs of the leading resorts, are no more; they are now converted to holiday flats. Also, there has been a proliferation of caravan sites, not always sited with care and consideration, although efforts to blend them in with the background have been tried recently. Again, the

traditional August break is no more: short breaks, weekend trips and days out are the ways that the tourist enjoys Dorset today. The visitor is as likely to come in the spring or autumn as in the summer, and wants to ramble or ride as much as to sit on a beach all day. This has brought a new kind of tourism, and new life to even isolated villages; cottage and farmhouse provide bed-and-breakfast to people wanting to escape their homes in overcrowded Britain and 'get away from it all'.

Readers with a long memory, who are familiar with the places shown in these photographs, will recognise some of the shops, views and perhaps individual people captured on film by the Frith photographers. It is strange to think that even the smallest child featured here, from some long-lost day in the 1950s, will be middle-aged by now. It is intriguing to imagine what happened to them all, and how they faced up to the latter half of a century where ways of life changed faster than any comparable period in history. Each person in these photographs will have had their own version of late 20th-century history, each version as valid as anyone else's. But those who stayed to grow up and remain in this beautiful county will know a Dorset that has, thank goodness, been spared the destruction and urbanisation that has beset so many other English counties.

ABBOTSBURY, THE SWANNERY BREEDING POOL c1955 A2002

Abbotsbury's famous swannery is home to over a thousands swans, and first became a popular day out in the aftermath of the Second World War. The swannery was in the care of Fred Lexster, a renowned swanherd and naturalist during the middle years of the last century.

ABBOTSBURY, THE VILLAGE c1955 A2005

Dorset villages such as Abbotsbury had changed little since the days of Thomas Hardy until the middle of the last century, when farming practices changed and tourism increased. This photograph could easily have been taken sixty years earlier with little difference in the view.

ABBOTSBURY, MARKET STREET C1955 A2025
Even in the 1950s cars did not dominate the roads of Dorset, except during holidays and at weekends. But as popular motoring increased, tea-shops such as The Flower Bowl, seen here, sprang up to cater for visitors and local residents alike.

ALDERHOLT
The Village c1960

Despite an increase in tourism, Dorset remains an agricultural county. Dairy cattle still crop the meadows around the village of Alderholt, and are still taken in for milking much as we see here. Drivers must proceed with care around Dorset lanes, particularly at milking time.

◆

ALDERHOLT
The Old Chapel c1960

Alderholt is a pleasant place to visit, surrounded as it is by the woods and heaths of the old hunting ground of Cranborne Chase. An ancient chapel once stood here, used by huntsman in Stuart times. This 'Ebenezer' chapel is a more recent replacement.

ALDERHOLT, THE VILLAGE c1960 A310013

ALDERHOLT, THE OLD CHAPEL c1960 A310003

ALDERHOLT, THE MILL C1960 A310007

Alderholt's mill was probably established in medieval times, though the present building is a hotchpotch of later architectural styles. During the latter half of the 20th century the mill was restored and opened to visitors as a craft centre and art gallery.

ASHMORE, THE POND C1960 A197302

Ashmore is a village of Cranborne Chase, with a splendid setting and a large pond that attracts a variety of birdlife. In the woods and heaths round about the patient observer can sometimes catch a glimpse of roe and fallow deer.

ATHELHAMPTON, THE HALL c1955 A198001

Tradition alleges that Athelhampton is the site of a palace of the Saxon King Athelstan, though the present house is largely Tudor. Athelhampton Hall was the location for the film 'Sleuth', which starred Laurence Olivier and Michael Caine. The Hall, which fortunately survived a bad fire in its East Wing in 1992, is open to the public.

BEAMINSTER, ST MARY'S CHURCH c1965 B40049

Until the commercial growth of towns such as Yeovil and Bridport, Beaminster was an important town for neighbouring villages. Its ancient linen trade had declined by the 20th century, and a nearby milk processing factory was one of the largest employers when this photograph was taken.

BEAMINSTER
THE SQUARE c1955 B40017
Beaminster is the 'sweet Bemmister' of William Barnes' famous Victorian poem. The town has acquired a popularity with Thomas Hardy fans, being the place where Tess of the D'Urbervilles finished her famous walk across the north of the county. Many literary pilgrims follow in Tess's fictional footsteps to this day.

BERE REGIS, THE VIEW FROM SCHOOL MEADOWS c1955 B480003

In the earlier years of the 20th century, Bere Regis had a reputation as the toughest town in Dorset, forcefully policed by the local constabulary. Popular belief is that the rowdyism was encouraged by the presence of the nearby Woodbury Hill Fair. Today, Bere Regis is a charming and peaceful village.

BLANDFORD FORUM, FROM ACROSS THE RIVER STOUR c1955 B282012

During and after the First World War Blandford became well-known as a military training area, with a large army base nearby. The poet Rupert Brooke trained here during the First World War. In the later years of the last century Blandford became the delightful shopping centre it is today.

BLANDFORD FORUM, THE BRIDGE c1955 B282024
Blandford has a long history as a market town, and for centuries sheep would have been driven over this ancient bridge to the famous Blandford sheep fairs. During the 20th century the old fairs stopped, and modern housing now covers much of the old market ground.

BOSCOMBE, UNDERCLIFFE DRIVE c1955 B151005
Boscombe spent much of its history in Hampshire, until bureaucracy reassigned it to the County of Dorset in the 1970s. A mostly Victorian town, Boscombe never quite became the spa town it hoped to be, despite the presence of mineral springs.

BOSCOMBE, THE PIER c1955 B151013
Boscombe Pier is a favourite place for a stroll for those on holiday. The structure was severely damaged during the Second World War, though it had been sympathetically restored by the time this photograph was taken during the following decade.

BOTHENHAMPTON, FROM THE SOUTH c1955 B157010

Bothenhampton was once an important village in its own right, but within the memory of the oldest residents it has become a suburb of Bridport. Too many people hurry through Bothenhampton, neglecting to visit its two impressive churches.

BOURNEMOUTH, THE BATHS FROM BATH ROAD c1955 B163015

Bournemouth did not exist at all until Mr Lewis Tregonwell built a holiday home in the middle of hitherto wild heathland in 1810. During the 19th century it remained a select resort for the well-off. In the happier days of the last century it opened its beaches to all, and a holiday in Bournemouth became an enduring event in many a Briton's memory.

BOURNEMOUTH, THE SQUARE c1955 B163031
In the latter half of the 20th century, Bournemouth not only maintained its reputation as a leading holiday resort and luxurious shopping centre, but became a university town and acquired city status. From one holiday home to a city in less than two hundred years!

BRIDPORT, SOUTH STREET c1965 B207070
As with so many Dorset towns on a main route, Bridport became clogged with traffic in the late 20th century. Its bypass has not really helped, and the town's streets are seldom as quiet as on this day in the 1960s. Bridport is best explored on foot, so park the car and wander around.

BRIDPORT
WEST STREET c1955 B207032

As its name implies, this lovely Georgian town was once a port, though its harbour is now two miles away at West Bay. In earlier centuries Bridport was famed for the quality of the ropes and fishing nets made there. In more recent times it has become the shopping centre for West Dorset and a development site for light industry.

BROADSTONE, DUNYEATS ROAD c1960 B735024

With the spread of suburbs around the larger settlements, functional but small shopping centres were established to cater for a growing population, with handy parking for the increasing number of car owners. Here, at Broadstone, are all the shops that would have been needed for a weekly grocery shop.

BURTON BRADSTOCK, THE VILLAGE c1955 B255019

The cliff line of Dorset breaks to give access to a small cove and the village of Burton Bradstock, with the River Bride gurgling away to the end of Chesil Beach. King Henry I once gave this village to the monks of Caen Abbey in exchange for England's crown jewels.

BURTON BRADSTOCK, THE VILLAGE c1955 B255079

The creation of an official long-distance footpath along the Dorset coastline has brought many walkers to Burton Bradstock. Several cottages in the village now offer bed and breakfast to weary ramblers.

CANFORD, THE POST OFFICE c1955 C396005

In the simpler days of the 1950s, village post offices across Dorset were places where the whole community might meet and were a vital lifeline to the outside world. The phone kiosk was essential, for the majority of Dorset homes did not then have a private telephone.

CHARMINSTER, THE VILLAGE c1960   C65012

CHARMINSTER
The Village c1960
Charminster dates back to at least Saxon times. Even in 1960, most of the residents would have been able to trace back their Dorset roots for generations, for there was not then the movement between English communities that there is today. As we can see from the prominent aerial, television had arrived - it changed the recreations of Charminster for ever.

◆

CHARMOUTH
High Street c1960
Until the construction of its bypass, most motorists sped through Charmouth on the busy road between Lyme Regis and Bridport, scarcely noticing this charming old village where Charles II hid after the Battle of Worcester.

CHARMOUTH, HIGH STREET c1960   C66027

CHARMOUTH, THE BEACH c1960 C66063

During the last half of the 20th century the beach at Charmouth became a mecca for the fossil hunter. Exploratory walks now take place from the heritage centre at the mouth of the River Char to help the visitor find and identify their own fossils.

CHIDEOCK, THE VILLAGE c1950 C87018

This evocative photograph shows cattle being rounded up at Chideock (always pronounced with the 'e' silent), on a peaceful day over half a century ago. This is still a familiar scene in the lanes of West Dorset.

CHIDEOCK, BRIDGE STORES c1955 C87082

Village stores soon began to cater for the new motorised tourist in the first affluent decade of peace. The Bridge Stores at Chideock sold everything the visitor could want, from ice-creams to picture postcards. Tourists with a little time on their hands could sample the delights of the tea parlour.

CHRISTCHURCH, THE RIVER c1955 C99078

Christchurch was actually an historic town of Hampshire when this photograph was taken, though it had an undoubted influence on nearby Dorset. This is one of the loveliest views of the priory church, said to have been built with the aid of a mysterious carpenter. It was named Christ Church in his honour.

CHRISTCHURCH, CHURCH STREET c1955 C99146

Christchurch has always been a busy town and a favourite place for shopping for both tourists and locals. It is interesting to note the variety of eating places in this photograph; at least two bear the title 'Ye Olde...' - a familiar designation for many business establishments during the 20th century.

COMPTON ABBAS, THE VILLAGE c1955 C398005

As if one Compton Abbas was not enough, Dorset is fortunate enough to have two: one is near Maiden Newton and is usually known as West Compton, and the other is near to Shaftesbury. Both are quite delightful.

CORFE CASTLE
THE VILLAGE AND THE CASTLE c1955
C160015

Originally the site of a Saxon hunting lodge, much of the present Corfe Castle, which gives its name to the stone-built village beneath, dates back to the troubled reign of King Stephen. This historic place at the heart of the Isle of Purbeck has long been a favourite place for the day-tripper coming from the nearby holiday resorts.

CORFE CASTLE
WEST STREET c1940 C160001
This is an excellent view of the fascinating shop front of 'J Cooper - Groceries and Provisions', with Mr Cooper's delivery van parked outside. Inside the main window a displayed poster warns 'Don't Help the Enemy, Careless Talk Costs Lives' - no doubt a relic from the Second World War.

DORCHESTER
SOUTH STREET c1955 D44020
It is a busy day in post-war Dorchester, which looks almost as though everyone in Dorset has come for their shopping. But apart from the motor cars and the considerable increase in visitors, the town has changed little since Thomas Hardy worked here as a young architect a century earlier.

DORCHESTER
High Street East c1955 D44013
The long main street of Dorchester probably
established its present line at the time of the
Romans, and has been used by travellers since. It is
still a popular route, despite the construction of the
unloved Dorchester bypass.

CRANBORNE, THE VILLAGE c1955 C694011
Cranborne Church, at the heart of the ancient hunting Chase, is one of the largest churches in Dorset. Cranborne and the villages round about were the residences of many local poachers until very recent times. Notice the advertisements for Mazawattee Tea and Spratt's Patent Dog Cakes on the building in front of the church.

EVERSHOT, MELBURY HOUSE c1955 E128017
Melbury House, the home of Lord Ilchester, was built in the 15th and 16th centuries, and was substantially enlarged in the 17th century. During the last century it has attracted tourists as much for its parkland as the house itself; many come to see the magnificent oak tree named Billy Wilkins by local people.

EVERSHOT, THE VILLAGE c1965 E128019
Evershot has changed little in character since the Tudor topographer Leland described it as 'a right humble towne'.
On the ridge nearby is the source of the River Frome - that beautiful Dorset brook that crosses nearly forty miles of
the county before reaching the sea.

EVERSHOT, THE VILLAGE c1965 E128022
Though the main roads are rather too busy for horseriding these days, the many country lanes, bridleways and ridge
paths make this method of transport an excellent way to explore the county and escape the pressures of modern life.

EYPE, THE BEACH AND THE CLIFFS c1955 E54045
This view shows Eype in the days before it was invaded by caravans and too many vehicles, though, as can be seen by the parked cars, some people had already discovered the delights of the beach at Eype Mouth.

EYPE, THE POST OFFICE c1955 E54028
In earlier times this wild coastline would have been known to the fishermen and smugglers who lived in these pretty thatched cottages. These properties with their well-kept gardens have survived into the new century.

FIFEHEAD NEVILLE
The Roman Bridge c1955
Roman remains abound in Dorset; many were excavated in the 20th century, including an impressive Roman Villa near this old fording place at Fifehead Neville. Finds can be seen in local museums.

FONTMELL MAGNA
The View from the Church Tower c1955
Fontmell Magna's church has a sad memorial to a victim of one of the greatest tragedies of the last century. In the churchyard is the grave of Alfred Simey, who died in 1931 of wounds received years earlier in the First World War.

FIFEHEAD NEVILLE, THE ROMAN BRIDGE c1955   F124002

FONTMELL MAGNA, THE VIEW FROM THE CHURCH TOWER c1955   F125002

FONTMELL MAGNA, THE POST OFFICE AND THE CHAPEL c1955 F125011
One local resident of two centuries ago was Philip Salkeld, who won the Victoria Cross at Delhi in 1857. Salkeld was mortally wounded blowing up a gate into the city during a battle in one of Queen Victoria's 'little wars'. His was a life of contrasts, indeed, beginning amidst the green fields of Dorset and ending in the heat of India. Salkeld's father was vicar of Fontmell for many years.

HALSTOCK, GENERAL VIEW c1960 H293004
Dorset has remained relatively unspoiled during the 20th century, retaining the delightful pastoral landscape that millions love. It is a land of woods, pleasant meadows, winding footpaths and quiet-flowing streams.

GODMANSTONE
The Smith's Arms c1955 G179003
The sign reads 'The smallest public house in England, originally a blacksmith's shop. King Charles I stopped here to have his horse shod. He asked for a drink and the smith replied 'I have no licence, sir'. So there and then the King granted him one'. The building measures some 20 ft by 10 ft.

HAZELBURY BRYAN, THE PLAYING FIELD c1960 H294009
The playing field at Hazelbury Bryan is mowed and rolled, perhaps in anticipation of a cricket match. How many sportsmen must have retired to this convenient hostelry after a hot and hard-fought sporting engagement?

HAZELBURY BRYAN, THE MEMORIAL c1955 H294012
Hazelbury Bryan is a scattered village, but the church stands on a prominent hilltop, so that it can be seen by villagers wherever they happen to be. Here is a fine memorial to those who have fallen in war.

HIGHCLIFFE
LYMINGTON ROAD c1955 H295021
Highcliffe is the most easterly parish in modern Dorset, famous for its views towards the Isle of Wight. The 1950s were the last profitable heyday for these small and diverse local traders before the arrival of supermarkets changed British shopping habits for ever.

HIGHER BOCKHAMPTON, THOMAS HARDY'S BIRTHPLACE c1955 H457004
Thomas Hardy, poet and novelist, was born in this cottage in 1840, writing his first few novels sitting on the window ledge of the upstairs right-hand room. Hardy took a keen interest in the fortunes of the property until his death in 1928. The cottage is now in the possession of the National Trust.

HILTON, THE VILLAGE c1955 H158003
A thatcher is at work, attracting an audience of appreciative youngsters. Thanks to the very large number of thatched properties in Dorset, this is one country craft that has survived into the 21st century.

HOLDENHURST, HURN COURT c1955 H296002

HOLDENHURST
HURN COURT c1955

The South of England has many fine stately homes, though a surprising number were lost during the 20th century. Very few are now the domiciles of one family; many have been converted into hotels or conference centres.

HOLDENHURST
THE VILLAGE c1955

During the latter half of the 20th century, Holdenhurst became more or less a suburb of Bournemouth and was blighted by some ugly new development. Holdenhurst's best attraction is its green, which has managed to survive the nearby and growing urban sprawl.

HOLDENHURST, THE VILLAGE c1955 H296015

IBBERTON, A DISTANT VIEW OF THE CHURCH c1955 I44002

IBBERTON
A Distant View of the Church c1955

The lovely old parish church of Ibberton is on a slope of the chalk downlands around the Blackmore Vale. It is likely that but for the efforts of one man, Lionel Seymour Plowman, incumbent at the beginning of the last century, this church would not have survived. Plowman took this almost ruined church and carried out a beautiful restoration.

IWERNE MINSTER
The Memorial c1960

Iwerne (pronounced Youen) Minster stands on the road to Blandford, and boasts this fine peace -rather than war - memorial. Iwerne lost its share of residents during the carnage of the First World War, and this memorial was erected in their honour. There is a carved figure of a soldier with reversed arms, and two nurses are remembered amongst the names on the plinth.

IWERNE MINSTER, THE MEMORIAL c1960 I65010

LANGTON MATRAVERS, THE VILLAGE c1965 L469032X
Langton Matravers acquired a reputation for quality education during the last century, thanks to its well-known preparatory schools. Many a schoolboy probably bought sweets at Priors' Village Stores.

LEIGH, THE VILLAGE c1955 L291008
One of Dorset's three ancient mazes stood at Leigh, though it had all but disappeared by the early 1900s. It is said that the maze was so complicated that it could take you all day to thread your way through it. Perhaps one day it will be reconstructed.

LITTLE BREDY, OLD THATCHED HOUSE AND THE CHURCH c1940 L293007
The pretty cottages of Little Bredy stand in a peaceful setting along the valley of the River Bride, despite having been in the front line of Britain's defence during the dark days of the 1940s.

LITTON CHENEY, THE POST OFFICE CORNER c1955 L468004
Litton Cheney has a charming collection of Stuart and Georgian cottages strung out along its winding lanes. Tiny brooks fill the air with the sound of running water, and the village church is a charming medieval survival. It is wonderful that such places have survived so well into the modern age.

LODERS, THE POST OFFICE AND THE VILLAGE c1955 L292005
This attractive little village in West Dorset stands at the junction of a number of ancient packhorse trails. Some of these, leading from the sea, were used by smugglers until well into the last century - or so one or two of the locals will tell you.

LONG BREDY, CHENEY ROAD c1955 L478002
A walk along the downlands around Long Bredy shows this to be a very old landscape, with barrows and monoliths from prehistory and ridge paths from more recent times. This lonely land was well protected by the Home Guard during the Second World War, when there was a great fear of invasion - just as there had been 150 years earlier during the time of Napoleon Bonaparte.

LULWORTH, THE COVE c1955 L112057
As car ownership increased, visitors to places like Lulworth Cove were in danger of destroying the very beauty they came to admire. The problem of cars in the Dorset countryside is one that has still not been resolved as we enter the new century.

LULWORTH COVE, GOING ASHORE c1955 L112022
Immortalised in literature and art, and the subject of a thousand picture postcards, Lulworth Cove is at the top of everyone's sightseeing list for Dorset. Day trips by steamer from neighbouring resorts were an essential part of a Dorset holiday in the 20th century.

LYME REGIS, BROAD STREET c1955 L121109
Lyme's most famous resident is the novelist John Fowles, author of 'The French Lieutenant's Woman'. The film version, which starred Meryl Streep and Jeremy Irons, was filmed here in the 1980s. One or two shops in Broad Street have retained the Victorian livery provided for them by the film's set designers.

LYME REGIS, BROAD STREET c1955 L121185
Broad Street boasts a great variety of inns and hotels. Famous visitors to Lyme Regis over the centuries have included Daniel Defoe, Mary Mitford, Jane Austen, Alfred Tennyson, the painter Whistler and Beatrix Potter. All found inspiration in the town and its beautiful setting.

LYME REGIS, LOW TIDE c1955 L121050
Lyme Regis straddles the border between Dorset and Devon, between two stretches of very unstable coastline. These produce a wondrous harvest of fossils, attracting fossil-hunters and geologists from far afield. Several fossil shops thrive in the town, for this has become quite an industry in Lyme in recent years.

MAIDEN NEWTON
The Mill c1960

Maiden Newton's mill spent a number of years in the 20th century as a carpet factory, in the same way that many of Dorset's old mill buildings had to find new uses in the modern age. The mill is situated on the site of many earlier mills.

◆

MAIDEN NEWTON
Dorchester Road c1960

Maiden Newton has been a much-appreciated centre for walking holidays in recent years, for many of the best villages and beauty spots on the Dorset downlands are within reach. A popular ramble is to the nearby Iron Age hillfort of Eggardon - immortalised by Thomas Hardy in his novel 'The Trumpet-Major'.

MAIDEN NEWTON, THE MILL C1960 M8044

MAIDEN NEWTON, DORCHESTER ROAD C1960 M8045

MARNHULL, THE VIEW FROM THE CHURCH c1955 M185024
Marnhull is in the midst of a rich agricultural area, with some of the best soil in Dorset for growing crops. Visitors are still shown the cottage that Thomas Hardy elected to use as the home of Tess of the D'Urbervilles. A number of new houses have been built here since Hardy's time.

MARNHULL, THE POST OFFICE AND THE VILLAGE c1955 M185032
The excellent quality of the buildings at Marnhull shows that this part of the Blackmore Vale was wealthy from agriculture. There are some fine stone buildings around the centre of the village - though around the edges some restored labourers' cottages can be seen.

MARSHWOOD, SHAVE CROSS INN c1955 M312007
The Marshwood Vale is not quite the deserted stretch of countryside it was early in the last century, 'with scarcely a habitation to be seen'. In earlier days, the village of Marshwood was of some importance, with a Norman castle and vineyard.

MELBURY OSMOND, THE OLD POST OFFICE c1955 M216005
Surrounded by beautiful woodland and rolling countryside, Melbury Osmond takes its name from an 11th-century bishop of Sarum. It has retained a pleasant peacefulness through the turmoil of the past century.

MELCOMBE BINGHAM, THE MANOR c1955 M217014

MELCOMBE BINGHAM
The Manor c1955
Melcombe Bingham's manor house dates back to the time of the Plantagenet kings, though much of the present building is Tudor. The Bingham family held the manor estate for several centuries, becoming a founding family of the United States of America.

MELCOMBE BINGHAM
Hartfoot Lane c1955
Much of England's social history can be explored by examining the manorial structure of villages such as Melcombe Bingham. It is interesting to note that the parish church seems to belong more to the adjacent manor house than to the village.

MELCOMBE BINGHAM, HARTFOOT LANE c1955 M217003

MILTON ABBAS
THE VILLAGE c1955 M80026
When the first Earl of Dorchester purchased Milton Abbey in 1752, he had the entire village dismantled and rebuilt further away from his new home. This picturesque village with its carefully tended gardens is the result of his quest for privacy.

MILTON ABBAS, THE VILLAGE c1955 M80008

MILTON ABBAS
The Village c1955
Recent residents may have had cause to be grateful
to Lord Dorchester for his patriarchal act. The
cottages of the new village were probably healthier
and more substantial than those of the
old settlement.

MILBORNE ST ANDREW
The Square and the Post Office c1960
Milborne St Andrew is a favoured village of the
ghost-hunter. A golden coffin is said to be buried in
the parish, but those who seek it are met with
thunder and lightning and the sight of a headless
funeral procession.

MILBORNE ST ANDREW,
THE SQUARE AND THE POST OFFICE c1960 M218014

MORCOMBELAKE, GENERAL VIEW c1960 M219010
Morcombelake, not far from Charmouth, originated in the early years of the 20th century as a retirement place for the elderly. The village lies under the shadow of Hordown Hill, a prominent local viewpoint.

MORETON, THE VILLAGE c1955 M308006
Moreton lies amid the remnants of the wild countryside that Thomas Hardy portrayed as Egdon Heath in his novels. Lawrence of Arabia, killed nearby in a motorcycling accident in 1935, is buried in Moreton's cemetery.

MUDEFORD, THE FERRY c1955 M106010
Looking out into Christchurch Bay, Mudeford remains the centre of Dorset's small-scale fishing industry, though leisure yachting has dominated from the middle of the 20th century. Mudeford has suffered from some hideous modern development in recent years, but retains its attractiveness for visitors who come to enjoy the sea.

MUDEFORD, THE QUAY c1955 M106011
Sheltered from the worst of the gales by Hengistbury Head, Christchurch's harbour empties into the sea between Mudeford's quays and sandbanks. Salmon are netted and crabs are caught by local fishermen, and dinghies are sailed by locals and holidaymakers alike.

NETHERBURY, THE VILLAGE c1955 N9024

NETHERBURY
The Village c1955

Here we see harvest home in the village of Netherbury. Perhaps the harvesters have retreated to the Star Inn, seen in the centre of this picture, after their hard day's work. It is not so very different in atmosphere to the pastoral novels of Thomas Hardy, written in the previous century.

OKEFORD FITZPAINE
The Village c1955

One of the prettiest villages in Dorset, Okeford Fitzpaine seems to have hardly changed since this photograph was taken nearly half a century ago. But how the Frith photographer must have disliked the intrusion of telegraph poles and wires in this artistic study!

OKEFORD FITZPAINE, THE VILLAGE c1955 O117002

OKEFORD FITZPAINE, HIGH STREET c1955 O117031
The brick-built houses show that this too was once a prosperous farming district. It is interesting to wonder whether the owner of the delivery van parked outside the New Inn was dropping off goods, or indulging in a pint of the excellent local cider?

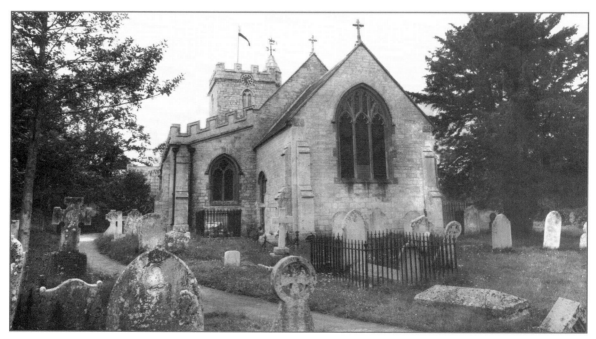

OSMINGTON, THE CHURCH c1955 O74025
Osmington is an ancient manor founded by the Saxon King Athelstan, though most visitors pass through the village to see the chalk figure of a later king, George III, carved on the downlands to the north.

OSMINGTON MILLS, THE RANCH HOUSE CARAVAN PARK C1965 O75047
Cheaper prices led to a heyday of caravanning in the 1950s and 1960s which has continued, though not quite on the same scale, to the present day. Love them or loathe them, caravan sites are now a common part of the Dorset scene, though most of the modern ones are much larger than the modest site seen here.

OSMINGTON MILLS, THE PICNIC INN, RANCH HOUSE CARAVAN PARK c1965 O75061
In the post-war years, many eating places were established to cater for the new influx of affluent tourists. Some were new additions to the countryside, while the majority was converted from former inns and cottages.

OVERCOMBE, 'THE NINETEENTH HOLE' c1960 O76001
Golf became an enjoyable recreation for a new generation of enthusiasts after the Second World War. Clubhouses, such as this one, became places to socialise and relive old golfing triumphs.

PIDDLEHINTON, THE NEW INN c1955 P230010

The River Piddle winds beneath the chalk downlands of Dorset, giving its name to several villages along the way before reaching the sea at Poole Harbour. Piddlehinton has been the property of Eton College for centuries. The sign above the door tells us that the landlord was Mr Albert Penny.

PIDDLETRENTHIDE, SMITHS LANE c1955 P231005

Some Victorian topographers were most offended by the word 'Piddle' and earlier guidebooks transformed it to the politer 'Puddle'. Hence, we get 'Puddletrenthide' and 'Puddlehinton'. But few locals today call these villages anything but Piddletrenthide and Piddlehinton.

PIDDLETRENTHIDE, THE POACHERS INN c1955 P231024
A good introduction to Dorset would be to follow the course of the River Piddle from its source to the sea, passing through some delightful villages along the way. There are many tempting places of refreshment along the route.

PORTLAND, THE BILL c1955 P91006
Portland, 'The Gibraltar of Wessex', as Thomas Hardy called it, is not an island but a peninsula. By the beginning of the last century, the island was famous for its great naval harbour, its prison, and the stone quarries that produced the fine Portland stone.

PORTLAND
The Bill c1955

Portland stone is renowned throughout the world as a prime building material. Sir Christopher Wren used this durable material for St Paul's Cathedral. In living memory, convicts from the nearby prison worked a great deal of the stone.

PORTLAND
Chesil Beach c1955

Chesil Beach forms an unbroken line of shingle from Portland to Abbotsbury; its stones are larger to the east than to the west. It has long been a hazard to shipping in bad weather. The novelist John Meade Faulkner depicted a typical Chesil storm in his novel 'Moonfleet'.

PORTLAND, THE BILL c1955 P91017

PORTLAND, CHESIL BEACH c1955 P91010

POOLE, SUNSET ON BAY HOLLOW ROCKLEY SANDS c1955 P72122
Rockley Sands developed as one of Poole's great leisure centres in the last half of the 20th century, and boasted one of England's first supermarkets to cater for the increase in visitors. This atmospheric photograph makes even a caravan site look attractive.

POOLE, THE HARBOUR c1955 P72054
Poole developed alongside the finest natural harbour in England. It still maintains strong links with the sea, having become a mecca for yachtsmen. Poole continues to function as a port, though as much now for leisure craft as merchant shipping.

POWERSTOCK, THE VILLAGE c1960 P233007
Once part of an ancient hunting forest and dominated by a castle, Powerstock huddles in its valley not far from the Iron Age hillfort of Eggardon, in the heart of West Dorset. Powerstock is a good holiday place for the archaeologist, for apart from the hillfort, there are prehistoric barrows, Roman roads and Saxon settlements nearby.

PUDDLETOWN, KING'S ARMS STREET c1955 P163027
A place of literary pilgrimage, attracting Thomas Hardy fans from all over the world, Puddletown is the 'Weatherbury' of Hardy's novel 'Far From the Madding Crowd'. Much of Puddletown was rebuilt in 1864, but the area around the church suggests the village that Hardy would have known in his boyhood.

PUDDLETOWN, THE SQUARE c1955 P163068
Until the 1950s, Puddletown was officially 'Piddletown', but - unlike the villages further up the river valley - the authorities changed this to the more acceptable Puddletown. Villagers call it by both names even today, sometimes mischievously to fox the tourists.

PUNCKNOWLE, THE WATERCART c1955 P120001

A cart delivers fresh water around the village of Puncknowle. The water came gushing from a grotto in the middle of the village. Unfortunately, this supply dried up soon after this photograph was taken, and the cottages were then connected to the mains supply.

RINGSTEAD, THE BAY c1955 R395013

Ringstead village had gone into a decline in the early years of the 20th century. The advent of popular motoring brought it back to life as a new generation of tourists discovered the nearby beach.

SIXPENNY HANDLEY, THE MAIN STREET c1955 S794002

Despite a 20th-century road sign which carried the name '6d Handley', the Sixpenny really has nothing to do with money at all. The village got its name because in Saxon times it was part of the Hundred of Sexpena. Locals just call their home village 'Handley'.

SIXPENNY HANDLEY, THE POND AND THE VICARAGE c1955 S794006

This is a timeless photograph. This fine study of a horse and cart at Handley Pond portrays a rural scene that could have been observed at any period during the last thousand years.

SHAFTESBURY
HIGH STREET c1950 S593007
The hill-top town of Shaftesbury, or Shaston as it is sometimes known, owes its foundation to Alfred the Great, showing much evidence of its Saxon origins. It has achieved popularity with visitors who wish to explore the far north of Dorset and the neighbouring county of Wiltshire.

SHAFTESBURY
GOLD HILL c1955 S593052
Gold Hill has been the location for several films and television programmes, including the 1960s version of 'Far From the Madding Crowd', and a much-broadcast commercial for bread. Despite its fame, Gold Hill remains one of the most beautiful streets in England.

SHERBORNE, THE ABBEY QUADRANGLE c1955 S112034

Sherborne is in some people's estimation the most attractive of the Dorset towns. It was once the capital of Saxon Wessex, and two kings, Ethelbald and Ethelbert, Alfred's brothers, were buried in its abbey. The town's bishops were expected to be warriors as well as theologians in those troubled times.

SHERBORNE, CHEAP STREET c1955 S112011

Cheap Street is one of Sherborne's ancient trading areas, and still fulfils that function today. Notice the cricket bat sign over Freeman's Sports Shop. Several excellent tea-rooms continue to prosper in present-day Sherborne.

SHERBORNE, HALF MOON STREET FROM THE ABBEY C1955 S112022

Sherborne is famous for its public schools, which give the old town an academic air. Pupils can often be seen threading their way around the old town. A musical version of James Hilton's novel 'Goodbye Mr Chips' was filmed here some years ago.

SHILLINGSTONE, GENERAL VIEW C1965 S443002

It is said that Shillingstone sent more volunteers to the First World War than any comparably sized village in Dorset. Many of them must have yearned for the peace and safety of these quiet meadows during their absence. Twenty-five never returned.

SHILLINGSTONE, THE POST OFFICE AND MAIN ROAD c1955 S443004
Earlier residents of Shillingstone had taken part in the Clubmen's Rebellion, an attempt by local people to keep the warring factions of the English Civil War out of the area. Oliver Cromwell, who considered that royalist spies were manipulating the residents, ended this interesting attempt at a peace process.

SHILLINGSTONE, THE CROSS AND MAIN ROAD c1955 S443007

Shillingstone remained a prosperous village for much of the 20th century thanks to the employment offered by a milk production factory and the convenient railway station. This lovely old cross was restored during that time.

SOUTHBOURNE, STREET SCENE c1955 S153059

Southbourne has an unfortunate place in aviation history as the scene of the air crash that killed pioneer aviator Mr Rolls, of Rolls Royce fame, in 1910. Rolls was the first person to die in a British air accident.

SOUTHBOURNE, THE PROMENADE c1955 S153123

Southbourne maintains an air of tranquillity compared to the bustle of nearby Bournemouth. The days when fishing boats were launched from the beach ended in the last century, when Southbourne dedicated itself to the tourist trade.

STOBOROUGH, THE VILLAGE c1955 S447003

Stoborough declined in size with the passage of time, but it was once as big as nearby Wareham, with a mayor and corporation of its own. Excavations in the middle of the last century found the remains of a Saxon chieftain prepared for burial in the hollowed-out trunk of a tree.

STOBOROUGH, THE KING'S ARMS HOTEL c1955 S447011

Both public house and petrol station prospered with the increasing volume of traffic on a road that the Edwardian topographer Sir Frederick Treves had described as 'a delightful walk'. Ramblers today now have to go further from the broad highway in search of peace and quiet.

STOKE ABBOT, THE VILLAGE c1955 S198004

One of the pleasantest ascents of Pilsdon Pen, the highest hill in Dorset, is from Beaminster and up through Stoke Abbot. Nevertheless, walkers eager to gain the heights of 'Pilson' should not miss the wooded heights of nearby Lewesdon Hill, a very enjoyable tramp.

STOKE ABBOT, THE WATERSPOUT AND THE VILLAGE c1955 S198008
William Crowe, rector of Stoke, wrote a paean of praise to Lewesdon Hill, which drew the admiration of William Wordsworth: '...of hills, and woods and fruitful vales, and villages, half-hid in tufted orchards, and the sea, boundless, and studded thick with many a sail'.

STOURPAINE, THE WEIR OVER THE RIVER STOUR c1955 S446029
There were several dramatic floods in the valley of the Stour in the last half of the 20th century, though its waters seem calm and restrained in this photograph. The Stour is another Dorset river well worth following from source to mouth, to gain a feel for this part of the county.

STOURPAINE, THE VILLAGE CORNER c1950 S446003
Stourpaine stands below the Dorset summit of Hod Hill, with its Iron Age hillfort overlooking the River Stour below.
At some point in its history, the fort was occupied by the Romans, for the coins of several emperors and other
imperial artefacts have been found there.

STUDLAND
The Bankes Arms Hotel c1955
The journey to Studland Bay has always been a favourite excursion for tourists from the nearby resort of Swanage. It is possible to either take the lanes or to follow the coastal path, admiring the views towards Bournemouth and the Isle of Wight along the way.

STUDLAND
The Ferry c1955
A car ferry sets out to cross the narrow entrance to Poole Harbour from Studland to Bournemouth. The neighbouring Studland Heath is now a national nature reserve, much loved by birdwatchers.

STUDLAND, THE BANKES ARMS HOTEL C1955 S226014

STUDLAND, THE FERRY C1955 S226017

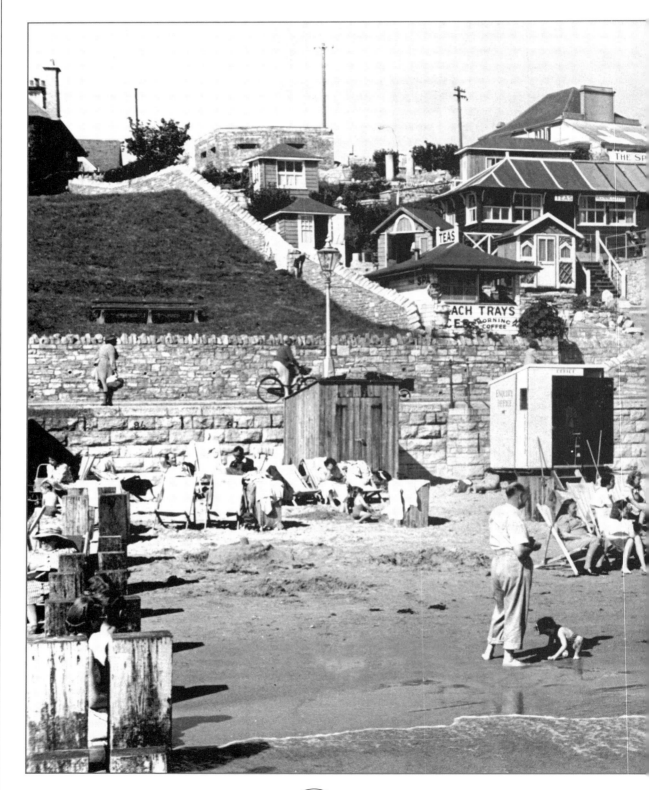

SWANAGE
THE SPA CAFÉ c1955 S239029
Swanage spent much of the 20th century developing as a holiday resort, though the town never seemed quite sure whether to try to appeal to the masses or the more exclusive visitor. Notice the bathing huts and the café that conveniently provided trays to take down on to the sands.

SWANAGE, TILLY WHIM CAVES c1950 S239023
Tilly Whim Caves, on the coast west of Swanage, are a strange mixture of quarrying and erosion. Tilly Whim was an attraction noted by early guidebook writers, who nevertheless deplored the graffiti left by Victorian visitors.

SWANAGE, THE SHORE c1950 S239247
On the right of this photograph can be seen Swanage Pier, built originally to facilitate the steamer trade to neighbouring resorts and the shipment of the much-prized Purbeck stone. Swanage remained a centre of the quarrying industry until well into the last century.

SWANAGE, THE GLOBE c1960 S239273

The Globe at Swanage was carved from a great mass of stone, ten feet in diameter and forty tons in weight. The Globe is placed to represent the position of the Earth in space, with four stone benches marking the points of the compass.

SYDLING ST NICHOLAS, EAST STREET c1955 S371004

Winchester College has owned much of Sydling for generations, ensuring a continuity of building and landscape conservation missing in so many Dorset villages. The charming Sydling Water flows through the village after a short journey from its source in the surrounding hills.

SYDLING ST NICHOLAS, THE CROSS c1955 S371019
The majority of Sydling's fine houses and thatched cottages have survived into modern times, making this one of Dorset's most interesting villages for the student of local architecture.

SYMONDSBURY, THE ILCHESTER ARMS AND THE CHURCH c1955 S246007
Just off the main road to Bridport is Symondsbury, a community of architectural gems, often missed by the modern motorist speeding between Lyme Regis and Bridport.

TOLPUDDLE, THE POST OFFICE c1955 T154005

Tolpuddle will always be an important place in English history. From here six farm labourers were transported to Australia in 1834 for taking an illegal oath in their quest for union recognition and better wages and conditions. This harsh treatment shocked the world, and the Tolpuddle Martyrs were eventually pardoned and allowed to come home. A small museum chronicles their ordeal.

UPWEY, AN AFTERNOON EXCURSION c1950 U13011

Looking at this photograph it would be easy to imagine an earlier period in time, but nostalgia for things past was already gaining a grip by the middle of the 20th century. And what a lovely way to see the countryside.

VERWOOD, THE CROSS ROADS c1955 V9001

Verwood was a hamlet attached to the nearby parish of Cranborne until the railway arrived just before the First World War. Speculators built many homes, and this substantial little town is now a favourite place for retirement.

WAREHAM, SOUTH STREET c1955 W173105

The streets of Wareham match the cardinal points of the compass, having been laid out in this fashion by the Romans. But its small museum remembers a later warrior, Lawrence of Arabia, who lived not far away until his death in 1935.

WEST BAY, THE HARBOUR c1955 W56043

Attempts by earlier generations to turn West Bay into a leading holiday resort never quite worked, though a great many caravans and holiday flats bear testimony to its popularity. In the last few years West Bay has served as the setting for the television series 'Harbour Lights'.

WEST BAY, THE HARBOURSIDE c1955 W56052

WEST KNIGHTON, THE RECREATION GROUND c1960 W341015
It is interesting to consider that these happy children are now middle-aged and perhaps reading this book! But what a lovely place to play as they grew up.

WEST LULWORTH, CHURCH ROAD c1955 W543004
Above Lulworth Cove is the village of West Lulworth. Much of the surrounding countryside has been used for military training since World War Two. The nearby village of Tyneham was taken over by the army; it was never returned to the villagers who were so speedily evacuated.

WEST LULWORTH
The Pond c1955

West Lulworth is a good starting point for a ramble along the Dorset coast, much of which remains unspoiled once you get beyond the range of the motor car. Even in 1955, West Lulworth was recording some of the highest visitor numbers in the county.

WEYMOUTH
The Beach c1955

The early use of bathing machines made Weymouth a popular resort for sea bathing, and the town has never looked back. It served southern England well both as a family resort and as a centre for touring during the last century - and still does.

WEST LULWORTH, THE POND c1955 W543006

WEYMOUTH, THE BEACH c1955 W76098

WEYMOUTH
THE PROMENADE c1955 W76222
Weymouth is made by its setting: the graceful conformation of Weymouth Bay has often been compared favourably with the Bay of Naples. No street in the town is more than a few minutes' stroll from the water.

WEYMOUTH, THE HARBOUR c1955 W76115
After Weymouth harbour was dredged and improved during Victoria's reign, larger ships joined the trade routes between the town and foreign ports. By the 1950s 700,000,000 tomatoes were imported here and 150,000 passengers transported to the Continent in a typical year.

WIMBORNE, EAST STREET c1955 W105008
The splendid Minster dominates the town of Wimborne, though there are many other buildings worth seeking out. Even in our superstore age, this town has managed to retain a number of little family shops.

WIMBORNE, THE SQUARE c1955 W105072
The Midland Bank and Woolworth's store draw the eye into this photograph of a remarkably traffic-free Square. Wimborne had a reputation, still not altogether resolved, of being a traffic bottleneck in the 20th century.

WOOL, WOOLBRIDGE MANOR c1955 W344032
Woolbridge Manor is another Dorset building with Thomas Hardy associations, for it was here that Tess of the D'Urbervilles spent her short and disastrous honeymoon with Angel Clare. The heathland beyond is now a tank training ground attached to Bovington Camp.

WOOL, SPRING STREET c1955 W344039

Wool originally grew up around Bindon Abbey, which was destroyed after the Dissolution. This straggling village has spent much of the last fifty years being dominated by a structure that proved to be as controversial - the Winfrith Atomic Energy Station.

YETMINSTER, VIEW FROM TARKS HILL c1960 Y30005

Yetminster rather resembles one of those lovely stone built villages in the Cotswolds, and has an unusual look for a Dorset settlement. The stony ground hereabouts led to the construction of stone walls as well as the usual Dorset hedges. In recent times the village gave a name to the much-loved Dorset folk-singing group the Yetties.

Index

Frith Book Co Titles

www.francisfrith.co.uk

The Frith Book Company publishes over 100 new titles each year. A selection of those currently available is listed below. For latest catalogue please contact Frith Book Co.
Town Books 96 pages, approximately 100 photos. **County and Themed Books** 128 pages, approximately 150 photos (unless specified). All titles hardback with laminated case and jacket, except those indicated pb (paperback)

Amersham, Chesham & Rickmansworth (pb)	1-85937-340-2	£9.99	Devon (pb)	1-85937-297-x	£9.99
Andover (pb)	1-85937-292-9	£9.99	Devon Churches (pb)	1-85937-250-3	£9.99
Aylesbury (pb)	1-85937-227-9	£9.99	Dorchester (pb)	1-85937-307-0	£9.99
Barnstaple (pb)	1-85937-300-3	£9.99	Dorset (pb)	1-85937-269-4	£9.99
Basildon Living Memories (pb)	1-85937-515-4	£9.99	Dorset Coast (pb)	1-85937-299-6	£9.99
Bath (pb)	1-85937-419-0	£9.99	Dorset Living Memories (pb)	1-85937-584-7	£9.99
Bedford (pb)	1-85937-205-8	£9.99	Down the Severn (pb)	1-85937-560-x	£9.99
Bedfordshire Living Memories	1-85937-513-8	£14.99	Down The Thames (pb)	1-85937-278-3	£9.99
Belfast (pb)	1-85937-303-8	£9.99	Down the Trent	1-85937-311-9	£14.99
Berkshire (pb)	1-85937-191-4	£9.99	East Anglia (pb)	1-85937-265-1	£9.99
Berkshire Churches	1-85937-170-1	£17.99	East Grinstead (pb)	1-85937-138-8	£9.99
Berkshire Living Memories	1-85937-332-1	£14.99	East London	1-85937-080-2	£14.99
Black Country	1-85937-497-2	£12.99	East Sussex (pb)	1-85937-606-1	£9.99
Blackpool (pb)	1-85937-393-3	£9.99	Eastbourne (pb)	1-85937-399-2	£9.99
Bognor Regis (pb)	1-85937-431-x	£9.99	Edinburgh (pb)	1-85937-193-0	£8.99
Bournemouth (pb)	1-85937-545-6	£9.99	England In The 1880s	1-85937-331-3	£17.99
Bradford (pb)	1-85937-204-x	£9.99	Essex - Second Selection	1-85937-456-5	£14.99
Bridgend (pb)	1-85937-386-0	£7.99	Essex (pb)	1-85937-270-8	£9.99
Bridgwater (pb)	1-85937-305-4	£9.99	Essex Coast	1-85937-342-9	£14.99
Bridport (pb)	1-85937-327-5	£9.99	Essex Living Memories	1-85937-490-5	£14.99
Brighton (pb)	1-85937-192-2	£8.99	Exeter	1-85937-539-1	£9.99
Bristol (pb)	1-85937-264-3	£9.99	Exmoor (pb)	1-85937-608-8	£9.99
British Life A Century Ago (pb)	1-85937-213-9	£9.99	Falmouth (pb)	1-85937-594-4	£9.99
Buckinghamshire (pb)	1-85937-200-7	£9.99	Folkestone (pb)	1-85937-124-8	£9.99
Camberley (pb)	1-85937-222-8	£9.99	Frome (pb)	1-85937-317-8	£9.99
Cambridge (pb)	1-85937-422-0	£9.99	Glamorgan	1-85937-488-3	£14.99
Cambridgeshire (pb)	1-85937-420-4	£9.99	Glasgow (pb)	1-85937-190-6	£9.99
Cambridgeshire Villages	1-85937-523-5	£14.99	Glastonbury (pb)	1-85937-338-0	£7.99
Canals And Waterways (pb)	1-85937-291-0	£9.99	Gloucester (pb)	1-85937-232-5	£9.99
Canterbury Cathedral (pb)	1-85937-179-5	£9.99	Gloucestershire (pb)	1-85937-561-8	£9.99
Cardiff (pb)	1-85937-093-4	£9.99	Great Yarmouth (pb)	1-85937-426-3	£9.99
Carmarthenshire (pb)	1-85937-604-5	£9.99	Greater Manchester (pb)	1-85937-266-x	£9.99
Chelmsford (pb)	1-85937-310-0	£9.99	Guildford (pb)	1-85937-410-7	£9.99
Cheltenham (pb)	1-85937-095-0	£9.99	Hampshire (pb)	1-85937-279-1	£9.99
Cheshire (pb)	1-85937-271-6	£9.99	Harrogate (pb)	1-85937-423-9	£9.99
Chester (pb)	1-85937-382 8	£9.99	Hastings and Bexhill (pb)	1-85937-131-0	£9.99
Chesterfield (pb)	1-85937-378-x	£9.99	Heart of Lancashire (pb)	1-85937-197-3	£9.99
Chichester (pb)	1-85937-228-7	£9.99	Helston (pb)	1-85937-214-7	£9.99
Churches of East Cornwall (pb)	1-85937-249-x	£9.99	Hereford (pb)	1-85937-175-2	£9.99
Churches of Hampshire (pb)	1-85937-207-4	£9.99	Herefordshire (pb)	1-85937-567-7	£9.99
Cinque Ports & Two Ancient Towns	1-85937-492-1	£14.99	Herefordshire Living Memories	1-85937-514-6	£14.99
Colchester (pb)	1-85937-188-4	£8.99	Hertfordshire (pb)	1-85937-247-3	£9.99
Cornwall (pb)	1-85937-229-5	£9.99	Horsham (pb)	1-85937-432-8	£9.99
Cornwall Living Memories	1-85937-248-1	£14.99	Humberside (pb)	1-85937-605-3	£9.99
Cotswolds (pb)	1-85937-230-9	£9.99	Hythe, Romney Marsh, Ashford (pb)	1-85937-256-2	£9.99
Cotswolds Living Memories	1-85937-255-4	£14.99	Ipswich (pb)	1-85937-424-7	£9.99
County Durham (pb)	1-85937-398-4	£9.99	Isle of Man (pb)	1-85937-268-6	£9.99
Croydon Living Memories (pb)	1-85937-162-0	£9.99	Isle of Wight (pb)	1-85937-429-8	£9.99
Cumbria (pb)	1-85937-621-5	£9.99	Isle of Wight Living Memories	1-85937-304-6	£14.99
Derby (pb)	1-85937-367-4	£9.99	Kent (pb)	1-85937-189-2	£9.99
Derbyshire (pb)	1-85937-196-5	£9.99	Kent Living Memories(pb)	1-85937-401-8	£9.99
Derbyshire Living Memories	1-85937-330-5	£14.99	Kings Lynn (pb)	1-85937-334-8	£9.99

Available from your local bookshop or from the publisher

Frith Book Co Titles (continued)

Lake District (pb)	1-85937-275-9	£9.99	Sherborne (pb)	1-85937-301-1	£9.99
Lancashire Living Memories	1-85937-335-6	£14.99	Shrewsbury (pb)	1-85937-325-9	£9.99
Lancaster, Morecambe, Heysham (pb)	1-85937-233-3	£9.99	Shropshire (pb)	1-85937-326-7	£9.99
Leeds (pb)	1-85937-202-3	£9.99	Shropshire Living Memories	1-85937-643-6	£14.99
Leicester (pb)	1-85937-381-x	£9.99	Somerset	1-85937-153-1	£14.99
Leicestershire & Rutland Living Memories	1-85937-500-6	£12.99	South Devon Coast	1-85937-107-8	£14.99
Leicestershire (pb)	1-85937-185-x	£9.99	South Devon Living Memories (pb)	1-85937-609-6	£9.99
Lighthouses	1-85937-257-0	£9.99	South East London (pb)	1-85937-263-5	£9.99
Lincoln (pb)	1-85937-380-1	£9.99	South Somerset	1-85937-318-6	£14.99
Lincolnshire (pb)	1-85937-433-6	£9.99	South Wales	1-85937-519-7	£14.99
Liverpool and Merseyside (pb)	1-85937-234-1	£9.99	Southampton (pb)	1-85937-427-1	£9.99
London (pb)	1-85937-183-3	£9.99	Southend (pb)	1-85937-313-5	£9.99
London Living Memories	1-85937-454-9	£14.99	Southport (pb)	1-85937-425-5	£9.99
Ludlow (pb)	1-85937-176-0	£9.99	St Albans (pb)	1-85937-341-0	£9.99
Luton (pb)	1-85937-235-x	£9.99	St Ives (pb)	1-85937-415-8	£9.99
Maidenhead (pb)	1-85937-339-9	£9.99	Stafford Living Memories (pb)	1-85937-503-0	£9.99
Maidstone (pb)	1-85937-391-7	£9.99	Staffordshire (pb)	1-85937-308-9	£9.99
Manchester (pb)	1-85937-198-1	£9.99	Stourbridge (pb)	1-85937-530-8	£9.99
Marlborough (pb)	1-85937-336-4	£9.99	Stratford upon Avon (pb)	1-85937-388-7	£9.99
Middlesex	1-85937-158-2	£14.99	Suffolk (pb)	1-85937-221-x	£9.99
Monmouthshire	1-85937-532-4	£14.99	Suffolk Coast (pb)	1-85937-610-x	£9.99
New Forest (pb)	1-85937-390-9	£9.99	Surrey (pb)	1-85937-240-6	£9.99
Newark (pb)	1-85937-366-6	£9.99	Surrey Living Memories	1-85937-328-3	£14.99
Newport, Wales (pb)	1-85937-258-9	£9.99	Sussex (pb)	1-85937-184-1	£9.99
Newquay (pb)	1-85937-421-2	£9.99	Sutton (pb)	1-85937-337-2	£9.99
Norfolk (pb)	1-85937-195-7	£9.99	Swansea (pb)	1-85937-167-1	£9.99
Norfolk Broads	1-85937-486-7	£14.99	Taunton (pb)	1-85937-314-3	£9.99
Norfolk Living Memories (pb)	1-85937-402-6	£9.99	Tees Valley & Cleveland (pb)	1-85937-623-1	£9.99
North Buckinghamshire	1-85937-626-6	£14.99	Teignmouth (pb)	1-85937-370-4	£7.99
North Devon Living Memories	1-85937-261-9	£14.99	Thanet (pb)	1-85937-116-7	£9.99
North Hertfordshire	1-85937-547-2	£14.99	Tiverton (pb)	1-85937-178-7	£9.99
North London (pb)	1-85937-403-4	£9.99	Torbay (pb)	1-85937-597-9	£9.99
North Somerset	1-85937-302-x	£14.99	Truro (pb)	1-85937-598-7	£9.99
North Wales (pb)	1-85937-298-8	£9.99	Victorian & Edwardian Dorset	1-85937-254-6	£14.99
North Yorkshire (pb)	1-85937-236-8	£9.99	Victorian & Edwardian Kent (pb)	1-85937-624-X	£9.99
Northamptonshire Living Memories	1-85937-529-4	£14.99	Victorian & Edwardian Maritime Album (pb)	1-85937-622-3	£9.99
Northamptonshire	1-85937-150-7	£14.99	Victorian and Edwardian Sussex (pb)	1-85937-625-8	£9.99
Northumberland Tyne & Wear (pb)	1-85937-281-3	£9.99	Villages of Devon (pb)	1-85937-293-7	£9.99
Northumberland	1-85937-522-7	£14.99	Villages of Kent (pb)	1-85937-294-5	£9.99
Norwich (pb)	1-85937-194-9	£8.99	Villages of Sussex (pb)	1-85937-295-3	£9.99
Nottingham (pb)	1-85937-324-0	£9.99	Warrington (pb)	1-85937-507-3	£9.99
Nottinghamshire (pb)	1-85937-187-6	£9.99	Warwick (pb)	1-85937-518-9	£9.99
Oxford (pb)	1-85937-411-5	£9.99	Warwickshire (pb)	1-85937-203-1	£9.99
Oxfordshire (pb)	1-85937-430-1	£9.99	Welsh Castles (pb)	1-85937-322-4	£9.99
Oxfordshire Living Memories	1-85937-525-1	£14.99	West Midlands (pb)	1-85937-289-9	£9.99
Paignton (pb)	1-85937-374-7	£7.99	West Sussex (pb)	1-85937-607-x	£9.99
Peak District (pb)	1-85937-280-5	£9.99	West Yorkshire (pb)	1-85937-201-5	£9.99
Pembrokeshire	1-85937-262-7	£14.99	Weston Super Mare (pb)	1-85937-306-2	£9.99
Penzance (pb)	1-85937-595-2	£9.99	Weymouth (pb)	1-85937-209-0	£9.99
Peterborough (pb)	1-85937-219-8	£9.99	Wiltshire (pb)	1-85937-277-5	£9.99
Picturesque Harbours	1-85937-208-2	£14.99	Wiltshire Churches (pb)	1-85937-171-x	£9.99
Piers	1-85937-237-6	£17.99	Wiltshire Living Memories (pb)	1-85937-396-8	£9.99
Plymouth (pb)	1-85937-389-5	£9.99	Winchester (pb)	1-85937-428-x	£9.99
Poole & Sandbanks (pb)	1-85937-251-1	£9.99	Windsor (pb)	1-85937-333-x	£9.99
Preston (pb)	1-85937-212-0	£9.99	Wokingham & Bracknell (pb)	1-85937-329-1	£9.99
Reading (pb)	1-85937-238-4	£9.99	Woodbridge (pb)	1-85937-498-0	£9.99
Redhill to Reigate (pb)	1-85937-596-0	£9.99	Worcester (pb)	1-85937-165-5	£9.99
Ringwood (pb)	1-85937-384-4	£7.99	Worcestershire Living Memories	1-85937-489-1	£14.99
Romford (pb)	1-85937-319-4	£9.99	Worcestershire	1-85937-152-3	£14.99
Royal Tunbridge Wells (pb)	1-85937-504-9	£9.99	York (pb)	1-85937-199-x	£9.99
Salisbury (pb)	1-85937-239-2	£9.99	Yorkshire (pb)	1-85937-186-8	£9.99
Scarborough (pb)	1-85937-379-8	£9.99	Yorkshire Coastal Memories	1-85937-506-5	£14.99
Sevenoaks and Tonbridge (pb)	1-85937-392-5	£9.99	Yorkshire Dales	1-85937-502-2	£14.99
Sheffield & South Yorks (pb)	1-85937-267-8	£9.99	Yorkshire Living Memories (pb)	1-85937-397-6	£9.99

See Frith books on the internet at www.francisfrith.co.uk

FRITH PRODUCTS & SERVICES

Francis Frith would doubtless be pleased to know that the pioneering publishing venture he started in 1860 still continues today. Over a hundred and forty years later, The Francis Frith Collection continues in the same innovative tradition and is now one of the foremost publishers of vintage photographs in the world. Some of the current activities include:

Interior Decoration

Today Frith's photographs can be seen framed and as giant wall murals in thousands of pubs, restaurants, hotels, banks, retail stores and other public buildings throughout the country. In every case they enhance the unique local atmosphere of the places they depict and provide reminders of gentler days in an increasingly busy and frenetic world.

Product Promotions

Frith products are used by many major companies to promote the sales of their own products or to reinforce their own history and heritage. Frith promotions have been used by Hovis bread, Courage beers, Scots Porage Oats, Colman's mustard, Cadbury's foods, Mellow Birds coffee, Dunhill pipe tobacco, Guinness, and Bulmer's Cider.

Genealogy and Family History

As the interest in family history and roots grows world-wide, more and more people are turning to Frith's photographs of Great Britain for images of the towns, villages and streets where their ancestors lived; and, of course, photographs of the churches and chapels where their ancestors were christened, married and buried are an essential part of every genealogy tree and family album.

Frith Products

All Frith photographs are available Framed or just as Mounted Prints and Posters (size 23 x 16 inches). These may be ordered from the address below. From time to time other products - Address Books, Calendars, Table Mats, etc - are available.

The Internet

Already fifty thousand Frith photographs can be viewed and purchased on the internet through the Frith websites and a myriad of partner sites.

For more detailed information on Frith companies and products, look at these sites:

www.francisfrith.co.uk
www.francisfrith.com
(for North American visitors)

See the complete list of Frith Books at:

www.francisfrith.co.uk

This web site is regularly updated with the latest list of publications from the Frith Book Company. If you wish to buy books relating to another part of the country that your local bookshop does not stock, you may purchase on-line.

For further information, trade, or author enquiries please contact us at the address below:
The Francis Frith Collection, Frith's Barn, Teffont, Salisbury, Wiltshire, England SP3 5QP.
Tel: +44 (0)1722 716 376 Fax: +44 (0)1722 716 881 Email: sales@francisfrith.co.uk

See Frith books on the internet at www.francisfrith.co.uk

FREE PRINT OF YOUR CHOICE

Mounted Print
Overall size 14 x 11 inches (355 x 280mm)

Choose any Frith photograph in this book.
Simply complete the Voucher opposite and return it with your remittance for £2.25 (to cover postage and handling) and we will print the photograph of your choice in SEPIA (size 11 x 8 inches) and supply it in a cream mount with a burgundy rule line (overall size 14 x 11 inches).
Please note: photographs with a reference number starting with a "Z" are not Frith photographs and cannot be supplied under this offer.
Offer valid for delivery to UK addresses only.

PLUS: Order additional Mounted Prints at HALF PRICE - £7.49 each (normally £14.99)
If you would like to order more Frith prints from this book, possibly as gifts for friends and family, you can buy them at half price (with no additional postage and handling costs).

PLUS: Have your Mounted Prints framed
For an extra £14.95 per print you can have your mounted print(s) framed in an elegant polished wood and gilt moulding, overall size 16 x 13 inches (no additional postage and handling required).

IMPORTANT!

These special prices are only available if you use this form to order . You must use the ORIGINAL VOUCHER on this page (no copies permitted). We can only despatch to one address. This offer cannot be combined with any other offer.

Send completed Voucher form to:
The Francis Frith Collection, Frith's Barn, Teffont, Salisbury, Wiltshire SP3 5QP

CHOOSE A PHOTOGRAPH FROM THIS BOOK

Voucher for **FREE** and *Reduced Price Frith Prints*

Please do not photocopy this voucher. Only the original is valid, so please fill it in, cut it out and return it to us with your order.

Picture ref no	Page no	Qty	Mounted @ £7.49	Framed + £14.95	Total Cost
		1	Free of charge*	£	£
			£7.49	£	£
			£7.49	£	£
			£7.49	£	£
			£7.49	£	£
			£7.49	£	£
Please allow 28 days for delivery			* Post & handling (UK)		£2.25
			Total Order Cost		£

Title of this book . . . .

I enclose a cheque/postal order for £ . . . .
made payable to 'The Francis Frith Collection'

OR please debit my Mastercard / Visa / Switch (Maestro) /Amex card
(credit cards please on all overseas orders), details below

Card Number

Issue No (Switch only)   Valid from (Amex/Switch)

Expires   Signature

Name Mr/Mrs/Ms . . . .

Address . . . .

. . . .

. . . . Postcode . . . .

Daytime Tel No . . . .

Email . . . .

Valid to 31/12/07

Would you like to find out more about Francis Frith?

We have recently recruited some entertaining speakers who are happy to visit local groups, clubs and societies to give an illustrated talk documenting Frith's travels and photographs. If you are a member of such a group and are interested in hosting a presentation, we would love to hear from you.

Our speakers bring with them a small selection of our local town and county books, together with sample prints. They are happy to take orders. A small proportion of the order value is donated to the group who have hosted the presentation. The talks are therefore an excellent way of fundraising for small groups and societies.

Can you help us with information about any of the Frith photographs in this book?

We are gradually compiling an historical record for each of the photographs in the Frith archive. It is always fascinating to find out the names of the people shown in the pictures, as well as insights into the shops, buildings and other features depicted.

If you recognize anyone in the photographs in this book, or if you have information not already included in the author's caption, do let us know. We would love to hear from you, and will try to publish it in future books or articles.

Our production team

Frith books are produced by a small dedicated team at offices in the converted Grade II listed 18th-century barn at Teffont near Salisbury, illustrated above. Most have worked with the Frith Collection for many years. All have in common one quality: they have a passion for the Frith Collection. The team is constantly expanding, but currently includes:

Paul Baron, Phillip Brennan, Jason Buck, John Buck, Ruth Butler, Heather Crisp, David Davies, Louis du Mont, Isobel Hall, Gareth Harris, Lucy Hart, Julian Hight, Peter Horne, James Kinnear, Karen Kinnear, Tina Leary, Stuart Login, David Marsh, Lesley-Ann Millard, Sue Molloy, Glenda Morgan, Wayne Morgan, Sarah Roberts, Kate Rotondetto, Dean Scource, Eliza Sackett, Terence Sackett, Sandra Sampson, Adrian Sanders, Sandra Sanger, Jan Scrivens, Julia Skinner, David Smith, Miles Smith, Lewis Taylor, Shelley Tolcher, Lorraine Tuck, Amanita Wainwright and Ricky Williams.

Free Print – see overleaf